MAR - - 2003

LIVES AND TIMES

Thomas Edison

Jane Shuter

Heinemann Library
Chicago, Illinois

© 2001 Reed Educational & Professional Publishing
Published by Heinemann Library,
an imprint of Reed Educational & Professional Publishing,
Chicago, IL
Customer Service 888-454-2279
Visit our website at www.heinemannlibrary.com

Designed by Visual Image
Illustrations by Sam Thompson
Originated by Dot Gradations
Printed and bound in Hong Kong/China

05 04 03 02 01
10 9 8 7 6 5 4 3 2

Library of Congress Cataloging-in-Publication Data

Shuter, Jane.
    Thomas Edison / Jane Shuter.
        p. cm. -- (Lives and Times)
    Includes bibliographical references and index.
    ISBN 1-57572-230-5 (library)
    1. Edison, Thomas A. (Thomas Alva), 1847-1931--Juvenile literature. 2.
    Inventors--United States--Biography--Juvenile literature. [1. Edison, Thomas A.
    (Thomas Alva), 1847-1931. 2. Inventors.] I. Title. II. Lives and Times (Des Plaines, Ill.)

    TK140.E3 S46 2000
    621.3'092--dc21
    [B]
                                                              00-035003

Acknowledgments
The author and publishers are grateful to the following for permission to reproduce copyright material: US Department of the Interior, National Park Service, Edison National Historic Site: pp16, 17, 18, 19, 20, 21, 22; Henry Ford Museum and Greenfield Village: p23. Cover photograph reproduced with permission of Rex Features.

Every effort has been made to contact copyright holders of any material reproduced in this book. Any omissions will be rectified in subsequent printings if notice is given to the publisher.

Some words are shown in bold, **like this.** You can find out what they mean by looking in the glossary.

Contents

Part One

Thomas Alva Edison was born in Milan, Ohio, on February 11, 1847. As a boy, he had a sickness called scarlet fever. This made him partly deaf.

Thomas loved doing **experiments** in his free time. But he started work when he was twelve. His first job was selling newspapers on trains.

In 1862, Edison was taught to use the telegraph, a machine that sent messages over a wire using codes. He worked as a telegraph operator at night, leaving the day free for his **experiments**.

Edison sold his first **patent** when he was 23. It was for a machine that sent **stock** prices by telegraph. He expected to get $3,000 for it, but he sold it for $40,000!

Edison started a business in Newark, New Jersey. His first job was to improve the telegraph. He also improved the telephone, so people could talk to friends who lived far away.

In 1871, Edison married Mary Stilwell. They soon had a daughter and a son. Edison worked hard and **patented** over 1,000 inventions during his life.

In 1876, Edison moved his business to Menlo Park, near New York. In 1878, he **patented** the phonograph. This was a machine that recorded and played back words and music.

Two of his workers made the first phonograph. Edison said, "This machine's going to talk." He recited "Mary had a little lamb" into it. The machine played it back.

In 1878, Edison planned to make an electric light. On October 21, 1879, his team tested the first lightbulb. They lit up the whole **laboratory**. Edison put on a public show.

Edison and his team then had to find a safe way to make a lot of electric power. Edison set up the first electric **power station** in New York in 1882.

Edison's kinetoscope was one of the earliest moving picture cameras. He used it to film movies in a building on wheels, called the Black Maria. The Black Maria could move to follow the sunlight.

In October 1929, Edison visited the new Henry Ford Museum. One exhibit was a **replica** of Edison's Menlo Park **laboratory**. Edison retired to New Jersey, and died on October 18, 1931.

Part Two

There are many ways we can find out about Thomas Edison and his inventions. Photographs show us what he and his family looked like.

There are also photographs of Edison's many inventions, and of his workers! This photo, taken in 1876, shows Edison's workers outside the Newark workshop.

Newspapers wrote about Edison's most exciting inventions. Other written records include lists of the films he made, and advertisements for his inventions.

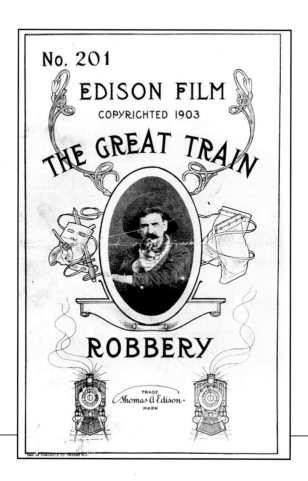

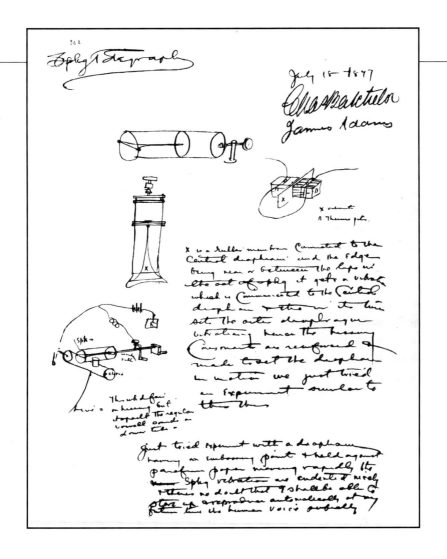

Edison used workbooks to sketch his ideas and work out inventions. He filled 3,400 workbooks, each with 200 pages. This page shows his notes on the phonograph.

Some museums have copies of Edison's inventions. This photograph shows Edison with one of the first phonographs. Now we can record sounds on machines that are much smaller.

This is one of Edison's first kinetographs. It used moving film to make the pictures appear to move. Edison's first movie showed one of his workers sneezing.

This is the Edison museum in West Orange, New Jersey. Edison retired here and built a workshop so he could keep on inventing. He kept improving the phonograph for the rest of his life.

This **replica** of Menlo Park is in the Henry Ford Museum, in Dearborn, Michigan. Everything is copied exactly from Edison's buildings.

Glossary

experiment trying out ideas to see what happens

laboratory place where people do experiments

patent signed paper from the government that says a person had an idea first, and is the only one who can use the idea to make money

power station place where enough energy is made to run a whole city and sometimes the area around the city

replica copy of something that is made to look exactly like it. You say *rep-lick-uh*.

stock small share in a business that people buy at a certain price and sell back for more money when the business is doing well

Index

More Books to Read

Levinson, Nancy S. *Thomas Alva Edison, Great Inventor.* New York: Scholastic, Inc., 1996.

Middleton, Haydn. *Thomas Edison.* New York: Oxford University Press, 1998.

Parker, Steve. *Thomas Edison & Electricity.* Broomall, Penn.: Chelsea House Publishers, 1995.